Beginning Classical Guitar

Nigel Tuffs

For online audio tracks scan the QR code
or go to fabermusic.com/audio

FABER *ff* MUSIC

Introduction

Welcome to *Beginning Classical Guitar!* This book is designed to be a formal introduction to the music and techniques associated with playing the classical guitar. The primary aim is to teach the student to read and understand music notation whilst gaining the best technique possible, creating a firm foundation for future studies. This method is aimed at both teachers and self-taught students.

For the professional teacher: This publication covers all the relevant notes and techniques required to play any Grade 1 (elementary level) piece across all major exam boards.

For the self-taught student: Do not try to move through the book too quickly – take your time. This cannot be stressed enough. Don't just play until you get it right, play it until you can't get it wrong. However, it is also important not to get bogged down; try to keep it fresh and interesting. Be hard with yourself. A teacher will persist until the piece is proficient, so do the same to yourself. Check your posture and how you address your instrument every time you sit to practise. Be prepared to endure setbacks; anyone can learn to play an instrument given the right tools, time and motivation.

Set aside a portion of time each day to practise (although a day off each week can be good), as familiarity is key. Your fundamental goal is to gain mastery over the instrument.

Each piece in the first half of the book includes both a demo track and a backing track for you to play along to and then as the book progresses, guitar guide tracks are provided so you can check your progress.

Nigel Tuffs

 All audio is available to download from fabermusic.com/audio or by scanning the QR code. Next to each piece is an audio symbol:

 indicates backing track audio

 indicates demo track audio

 indicates real guitar guide audio

All pieces unless otherwise indicated are composed or arranged by Nigel Tuffs. MIDI tracks by Jan Halen.
Many thanks to Maria Fragkiadaki, Jan Halen, Chris Hargrave, Ady Johnson, Sébastien Vachez and my editor, Emily Bevington.

© 2021 by Faber Music Ltd
First published by Faber Music Ltd
Bloomsbury House, 74–77 Great Russell Street, London WC1B 3DA
Cover design by Chloë Alexander Design
Cover image: Paulino Bernabé by kind permission from Siccas Guitars (www.siccasguitars.com)
Page design and illustration by Elizabeth Ogden
Printed in England by Caligraving Ltd
All rights reserved

ISBN10: 0-571-54199-2
EAN13: 978-0-571-54199-7

To buy Faber Music publications or to find out about the full range of titles available
please contact your local music retailer or Faber Music sales enquiries:

Faber Music Ltd, Burnt Mill, Elizabeth Way, Harlow CM20 2HX
Tel: +44 (0) 1279 82 89 82
fabermusic.com

The classical guitar

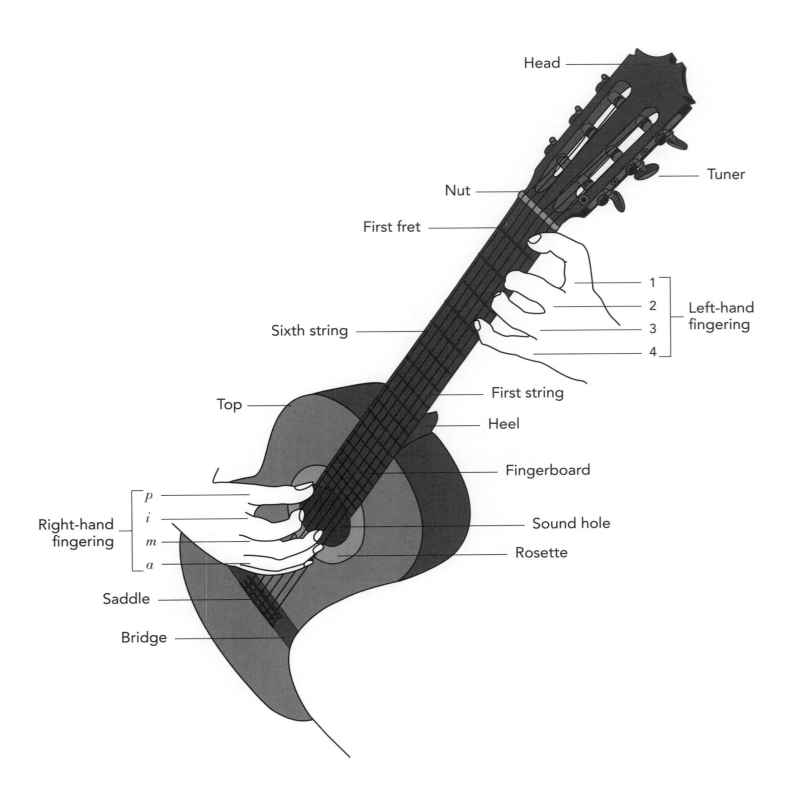

Head

Tuner

Nut

First fret

1
2
3
4

Left-hand
fingering

Sixth string

First string

Top

Heel

Fingerboard

p
i
m
a

Right-hand
fingering

Sound hole

Rosette

Saddle

Bridge

Sitting position and posture

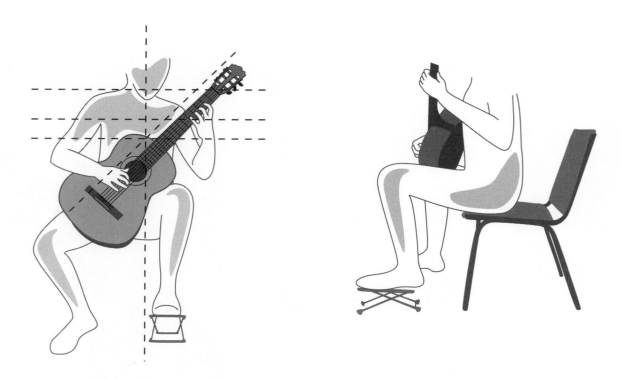

Study the above illustrations carefully and try to match the players' positions. Note the use of a footstool to raise the left leg and instrument to an angle of 45°. There are also guitar rests available that attach to the instrument to achieve the same result, enabling you to keep both feet on the floor for better overall posture.

Tuning your instrument

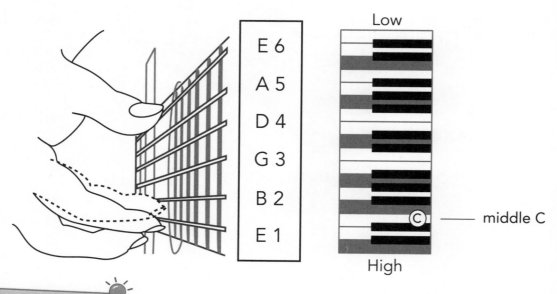

A tuning track is also available to download.

Preparing to play: the rest stroke or *apoyando*

The pictures below show the preparation and execution of a rest stroke, or *apoyando* as it will be referred to in this book. This is not the only method of effectively striking a string but it is the foundation of any right-hand technique and must become second nature before other techniques are learned. Pay careful attention to the position of both the fingers and the hand in relation to the instrument.

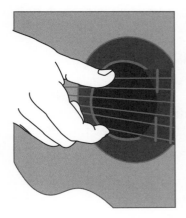

Preparation

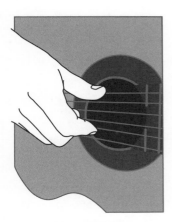

Execution

Executing the *apoyando*

1. To perform an *apoyando*, first place your thumb on string 6 (the thickest and lowest sounding string). Make sure it is forward of the fingers and producing an 'X' shape.

2. Now place your index finger on string 1 so that the string is on the fingertip adjacent to the nail. Using the knuckle as the source of the movement, pull across towards the thumb coming to rest on string 2 at the end of the stroke. Repeat several times.

3. Now try alternating with the middle finger so you are 'walking'.

4. Repeat, counting (for each stroke) to 4 each time:

   i m i m| i m i m
   1 2 3 4 | 1 2 3 4

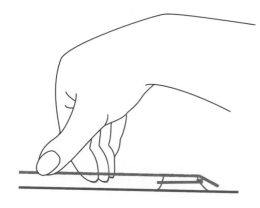

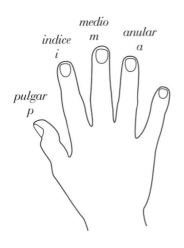

Music notation

Bar (Measure)   Stave (Staff)

Barline   Final barline
(End of piece)

In its most basic form, music notation is very simple. Each note has just two jobs to perform:

Pitch: how high or low the note is

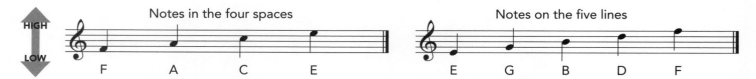

HIGH   Notes in the four spaces   Notes on the five lines

LOW

F   A   C   E   E   G   B   D   F

When notes are below the middle line of the stave (staff), the stems point downwards. When notes are above the middle line of the stave (staff), the stems point upwards. The note B, on the middle line, can have its stem pointing either up or down.

Rhythm: how long or short a note is

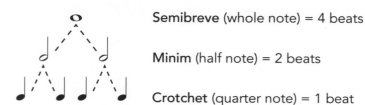

Semibreve (whole note) = 4 beats

Minim (half note) = 2 beats

Crotchet (quarter note) = 1 beat

The **time signature** tells you how to organise the beats in the bar (measure):

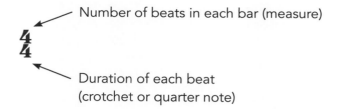

Number of beats in each bar (measure)

Duration of each beat
(crotchet or quarter note)

The following exercise should be played using the *apoyando* (rest stroke) method outlined on page 5. Count four beats in a bar (measure).

This exercise uses the note E
(see page 7).

Walking fingers

Count: 1   2   3   4   1   2   3   4   1   2   3   4   1   2   3   4

New notes: E, B and G

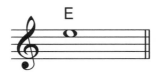
E

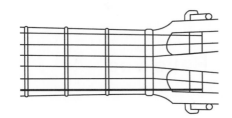

Rhythm exercises on E

Count: 1 2 3 4 1 2 3 4 1 2 3 4 1 2 3 4

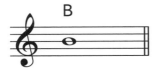
B

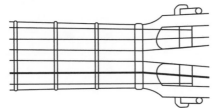

Rhythm exercises on B

Count: 1 2 3 4 1 2 3 4 1 2 3 4 1 2 3 4

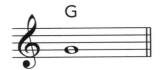
G

Always count yourself in: 1 2 3 4 PLAY!
This will help establish a solid tempo (speed).

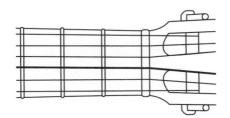

Rhythm exercise on G

Count: 1 2 3 4 1 2 3 4 1 2 3 4 1 2 3 4

1 2 3 4 1 2 3 4 1 2 3 4 1 2 3 4

The following pieces contain a combination of the notes and rhythms learnt so far. Right-hand fingering is given at the start, and if you keep alternating in the same way, it should match the fingering given at the end of the piece.

> Refer back to the diagram on page 3 to recap the right-hand fingering.

Belle vue

Sometimes pieces will have letters written above the stave (staff). These are called chords and are for a teacher or accompanist to play. At other times an accompanying part will be written out.

> New note value: $\bullet$ = 3 beats

Preview

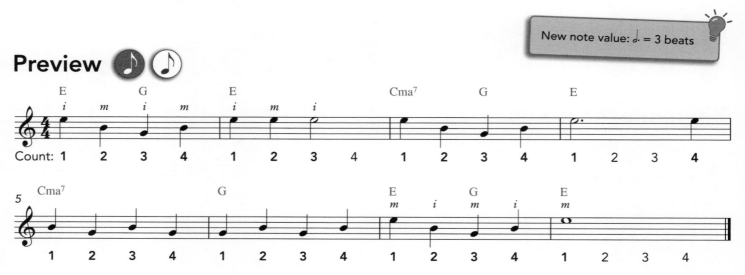

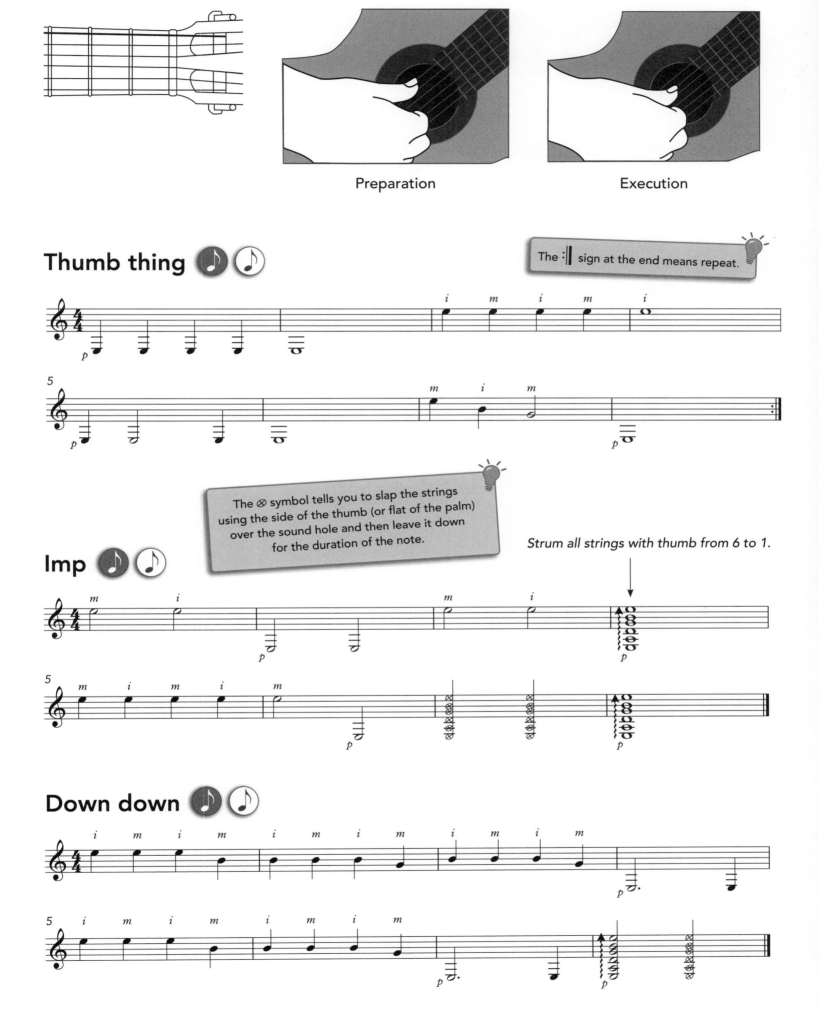

Preparation

Execution

Thumb thing

The :|| sign at the end means repeat.

Imp

The ⊗ symbol tells you to slap the strings using the side of the thumb (or flat of the palm) over the sound hole and then leave it down for the duration of the note.

Strum all strings with thumb from 6 to 1.

Down down

First performance piece

When two instrumentalists play together, their individual parts are joined by a bracket on the left. In this book, the accompanying part will always be smaller, below the solo part.

Prelude

This is a metronome mark – an indication of the tempo (speed). Set your metronome to the speed written below to give you 90 beats per minute.

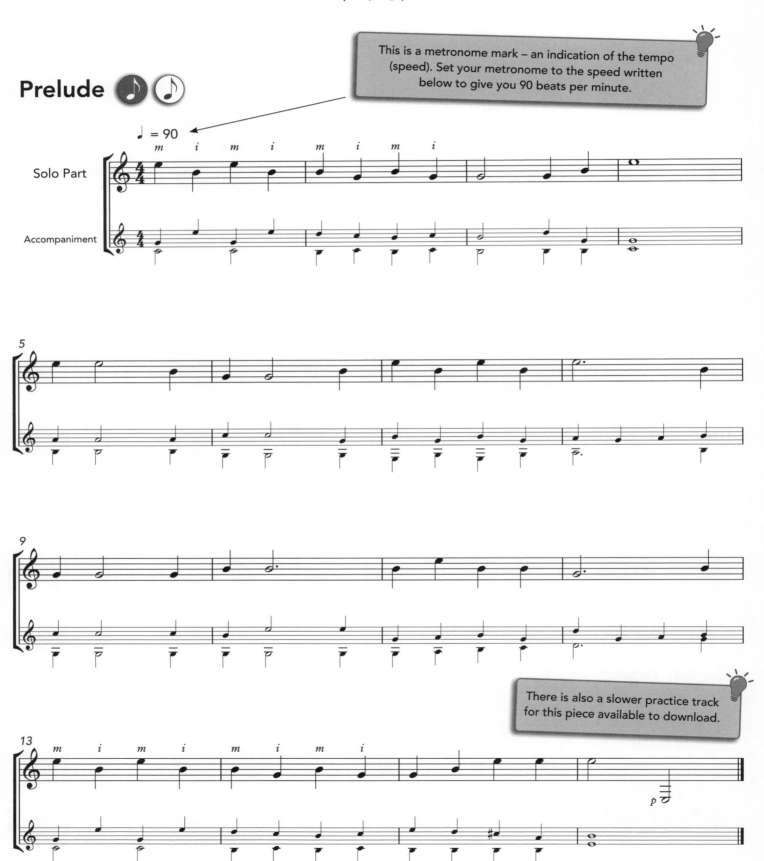

There is also a slower practice track for this piece available to download.

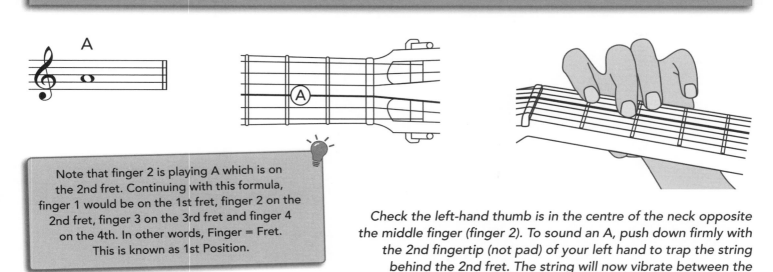

New note: A

Note that finger 2 is playing A which is on the 2nd fret. Continuing with this formula, finger 1 would be on the 1st fret, finger 2 on the 2nd fret, finger 3 on the 3rd fret and finger 4 on the 4th. In other words, Finger = Fret. This is known as 1st Position.

Check the left-hand thumb is in the centre of the neck opposite the middle finger (finger 2). To sound an A, push down firmly with the 2nd fingertip (not pad) of your left hand to trap the string behind the 2nd fret. The string will now vibrate between the saddle and fret 2. Refer back to page 3 for left-hand fingerings.

Exercise

Before each practice session use the right-hand exercises from page 7 as warm-ups, then play four of each of the notes above, then repeat. When you see an '0' this indicates an open string.

Gabby

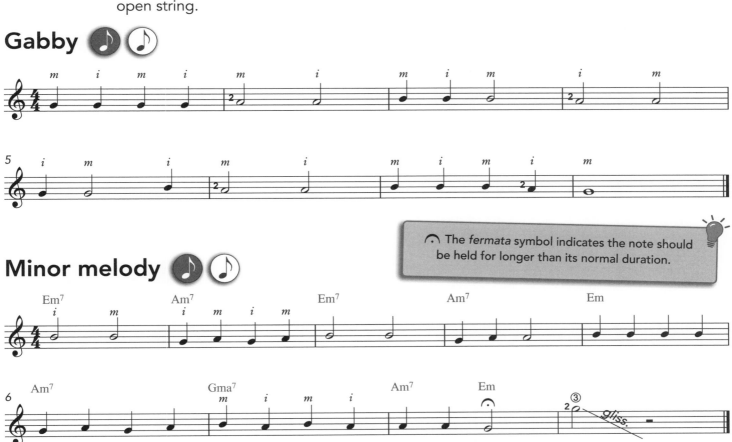

⌢ The *fermata* symbol indicates the note should be held for longer than its normal duration.

Minor melody

gliss. (glissando) = slide. Find fret number 12 on the G string, play the note, then slide down keeping some pressure but not too much.

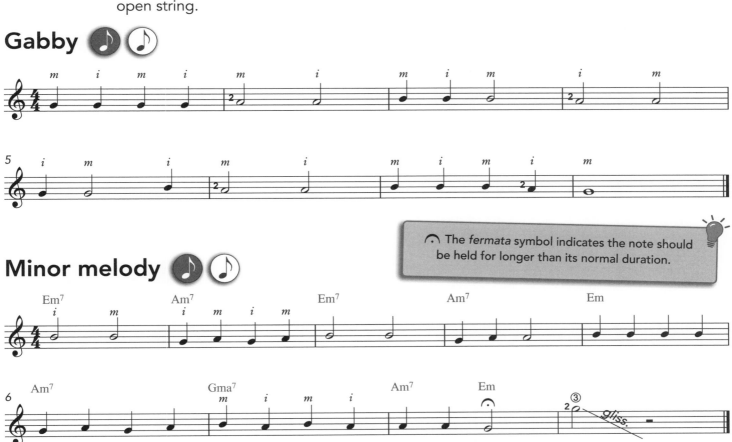

New note: C

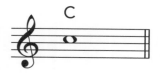
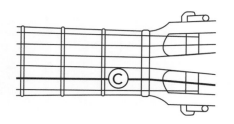
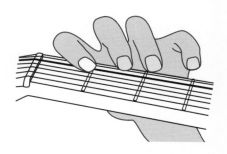

First, start with the exercises and when you feel confident, move onto the pieces.

Exercise 1

Exercise 2

The beach 🎵 🎵

> This piece is in $\frac{2}{4}$. The top number indicates there are 2 beats in a bar (measure) and the bottom number that they are all crochets (quarter notes).

Two time 🎵 🎵

New note: D

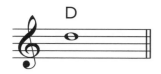
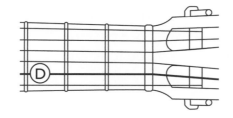
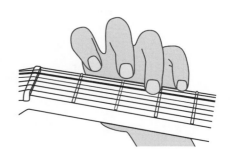

Before each practice session, use the following exercise as a warm-up. Then repeat, playing each note four times. Alternate the fingering as you play.

Exercise

G   A   B   C   D   E   D   C   B   A   G

Gabby 2

This piece can be played as a duet with Gabby (page 11).

Just skip

D.C. stands for Da Capo which means return to the beginning and al Fine means stop where it says Fine.

Ties

A tie does exactly what it says – it ties, or joins, two notes of the same pitch. In the first piece, two minims (half notes) have been tied together to create a 4-beat note in $\frac{2}{4}$. Play the first note and then let it ring on for the duration of the second.

Step by step

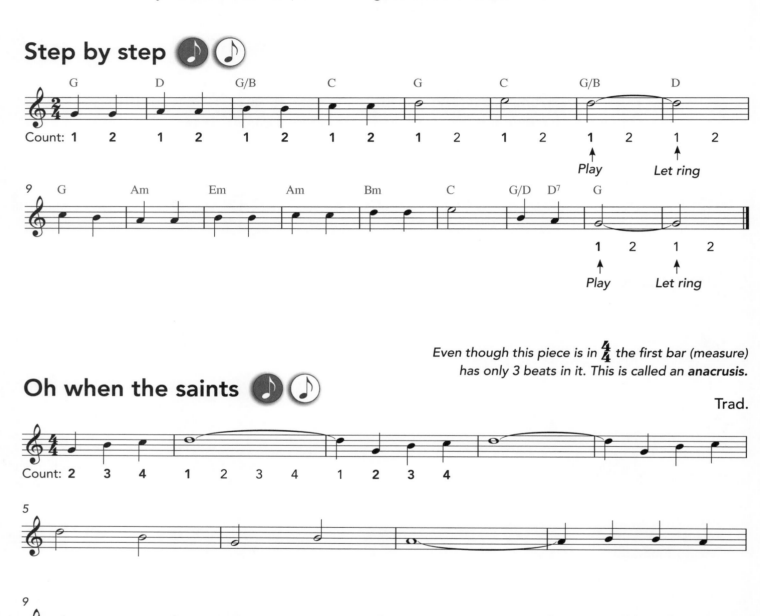

Oh when the saints

*Even though this piece is in $\frac{4}{4}$ the first bar (measure) has only 3 beats in it. This is called an **anacrusis**.*

Trad.

There is also a slower practice track for this piece available to download.

New notes: F and G

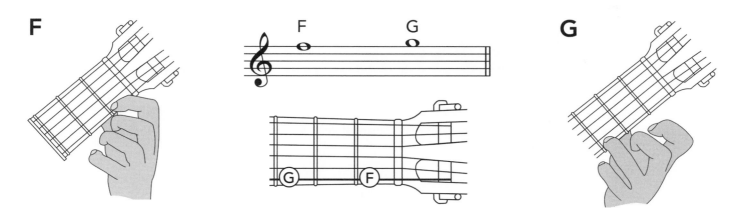

This exercise is in $\frac{3}{4}$. The top number indicates that there are three beats in a bar (measure) and the bottom number that they are all crotchets (quarter notes).

Exercise

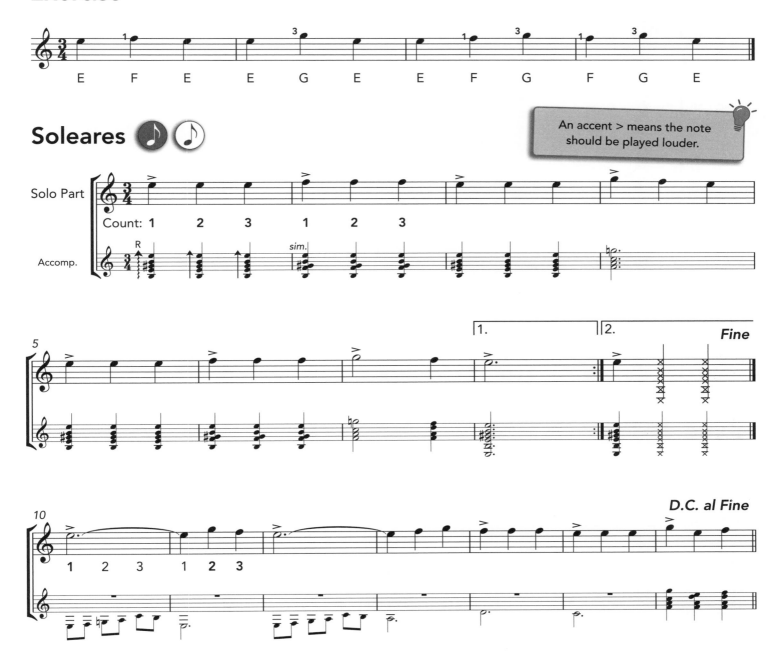

Soleares

An accent > means the note should be played louder.

Mixolydian mode

The Mixolydian mode is the first full seven-note scale in this book. It can be used as a warm-up exercise as follows:

- Play the scale several times paying close attention to the left hand (using just your thumb in the right hand to avoid the distraction of *i m i m*).
- Now add the right hand making sure you alternate (walk) your right-hand fingering.
- Play four of each note, then three, then two and finally one, making sure you are still walking.

Hyper mix

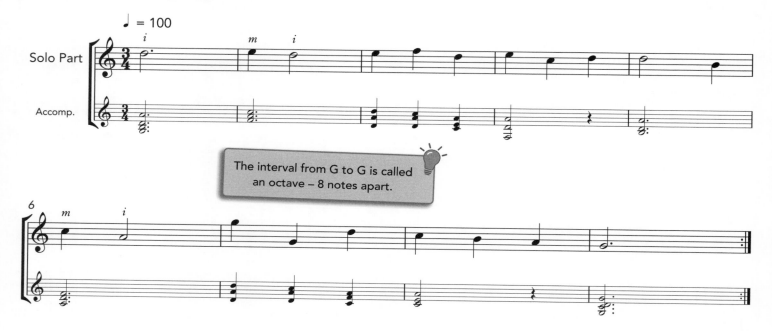

The interval from G to G is called an octave – 8 notes apart.

Kyrie

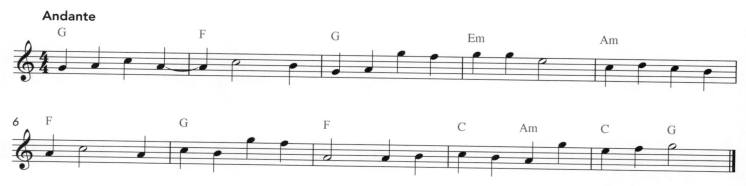

Dynamics

Near and far

Folk

Accidentals

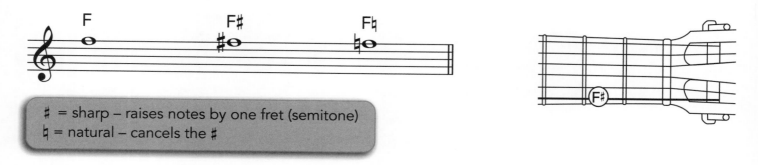

> ♯ = sharp – raises notes by one fret (semitone)
> ♮ = natural – cancels the ♯

Exercise

You may notice the following scale is the same as the Mixolydian mode (see page 16) but with an F♯ (a raised 7th). Now use this scale as a warm-up instead of the Mixolydian mode.

G major scale

The single sharp sign before the time signature $\frac{4}{4}$ indicates that every F is sharp unless a natural sign cancels it. It is known as a **key signature**.

Green lanes 🎵

> The 2° tells you to play *mp* on the repeat.

Sign	Name	Relative length	In 4/4 time	Rest
o	Semibreve	Whole note	4 beats	▬
♩(minim)	Minim	Half note	2 beats	▬
♩	Crotchet	Quarter note	1 beat	𝄽

To create the silence needed to play a rest simply start with *m* then on the next beat place *i* on string 1 to stop the string vibrating; *i* is now 'prepared' and ready to execute the next note of E.

Exercise 1

Count: **1** (2) **3** (4) **1** 2 (3) (4) **1** (2) (3) (4) (1) **2** (3) (4)

Exercise 2

Count: **1** (2) **3** (4) **1** (2) **3** (4) **1** (2) **3** (4) **1** (2) **3** (4)

B roads

The number shows you which string the notes should be played on.

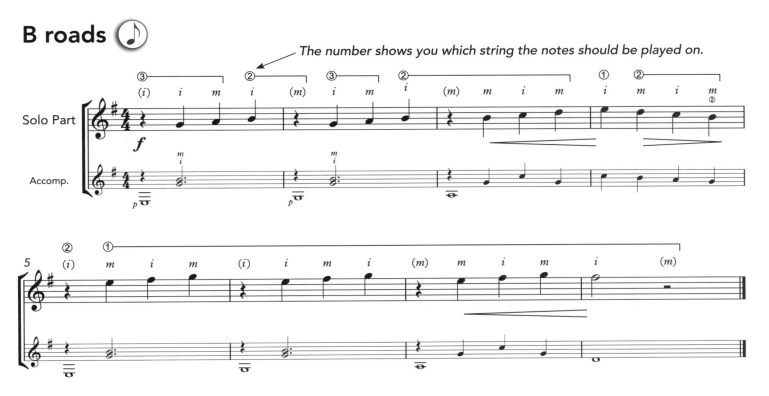

This piece can be played as a B section with **Green lanes** as A (AABA).

Arpeggios

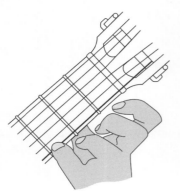

An arpeggio comprises the notes of a chord heard one after another.

So far, finger 4 has not been used (see 'Finger = Fret' on page 11) but to make the following arpeggio smoother, finger 4 plays the top note of G. (Look out for further use of finger 4 on G as the book progresses.)

The G major arpeggio below can be played *lessez vibrer (l.v.)* – letting the notes ring-over where possible – by keeping fingers 3 and 4 down throughout.

G major arpeggio

What a game

Try writing in your own dynamics.

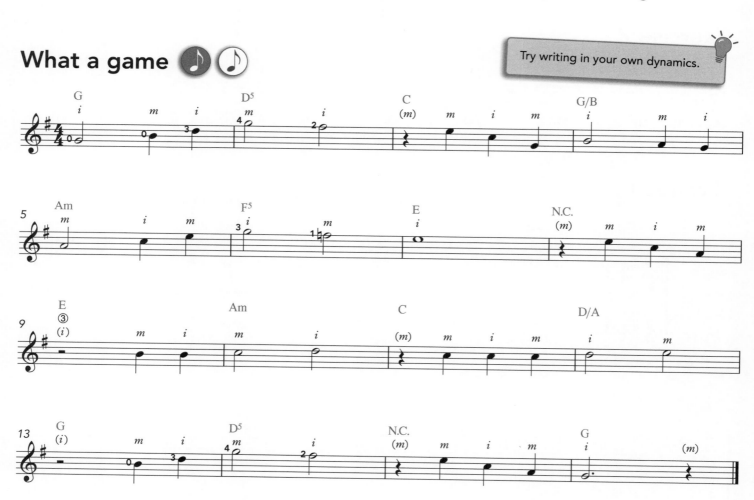

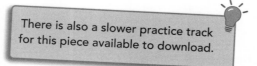

There is also a slower practice track for this piece available to download.

Bass notes: strings 6, 5 and 4

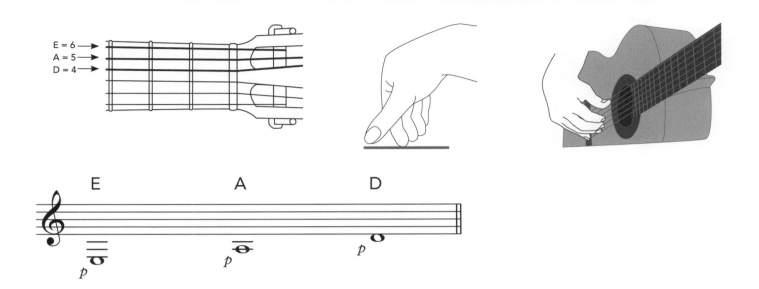

Refer back to 'Tuning your instrument' on page 4 and review the illustrations on page 9 of the preparation and execution of *apoyando* using the thumb before you start. To produce a rest with the thumb simply place it back on the bass string to stop it ringing on.

Exercise 🎵

Music in two parts

Now bass notes have been introduced fully, you'll see that the music is in two parts or voices. All the notes to be played with the fingers have upward stems and all those to be played by the thumb have downward stems. Note that both the fingers and the thumb have their own rests, too.

New note: A

The graphic on the left shows a change in position for the left hand. So far, every note stopped with the left hand has been in 1st position (finger = fret) indicated by the Roman numeral I. To reach top A, move your hand up so that the 1st finger is over the 3rd fret, and the 3rd finger can play the 5th fret note of A – this is called 3rd position. When descending, G is played with finger 1. The hand then moves back to 1st position to play F.

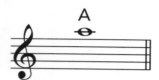

A natural minor scale

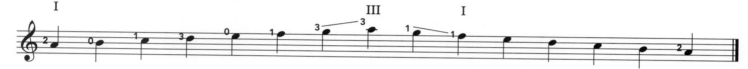

A minor arpeggio

Pavane and Galliard

In the following piece, use a *sostenuto* (sustained) approach and simply let all the notes ring on. (The performance technique is left usually to the judgement of the performer but this book will cover as many approaches to performance and notation as possible.)

Pavane

Lean your fingers on the top string at this point.

rall. = rallentando: gradually slowing down

The first note of Galliard is another example of an *anacrusis*.

Galliard

Note that the final bar has only two beats to make up for the single crotchet (quarter note) anacrusis.

New note: G♯

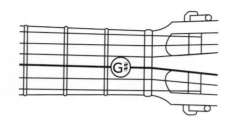

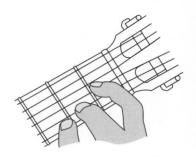

This piece brings together everything you have learnt so far.

The mystery

Let ring for 2 seconds.

The free stroke or *tirando*

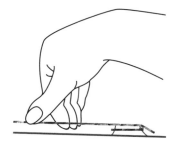

Thumb: Like the *apoyando* the thumb begins by resting on string 6; but unlike the *apoyando*, where the thumb follows through and rests on the adjacent string, in *tirando* the thumb moves forward and away from the string.

Fingers: Like the *apoyando* the index finger begins by resting on string 1; but unlike the *apoyando*, where the fingers follow through and rest on the adjacent string, in *tirando* the fingers move towards the thumb and away from the string.

Thumb   Fingers

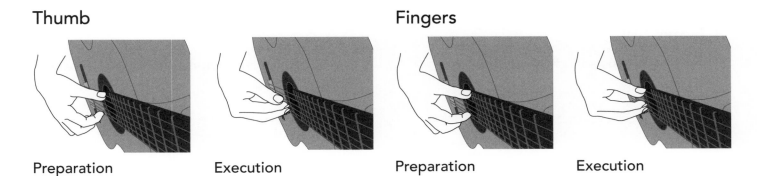

Preparation   Execution   Preparation   Execution

Plant and play

Plant: Place *p* on string 6 and *i m a* on strings 3, 2 and 1. The strings should be on the fingertips – close to the fingernails, but not touching.

Play: Execute a *tirando* playing *p i m a* simultaneously.

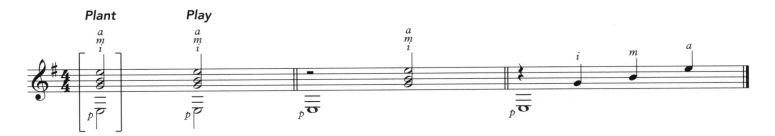

The second bar separates the thumb from the fingers and the third bar has all the digits moving one after another in the order *p i m a*.

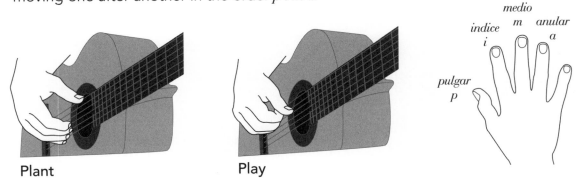

Plant   Play

New note: G

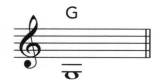
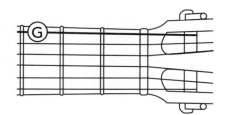
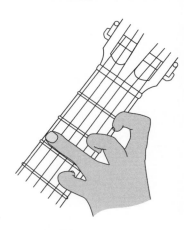

Chord

The simultaneous sounding of more than one note.

Stem down for the thumb

Arpeggio

The sounding of the notes of a chord in succession: a broken chord.

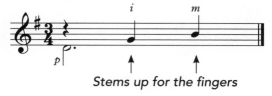

Stems up for the fingers

Chord and arpeggio exercise

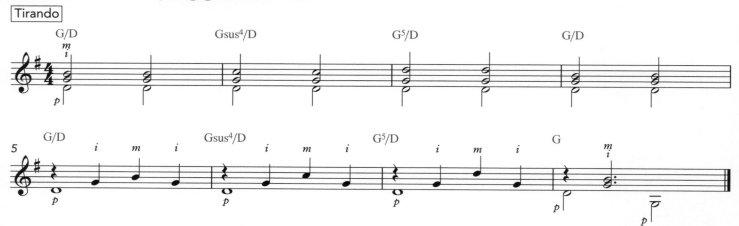

Chord and arpeggio exercise 2

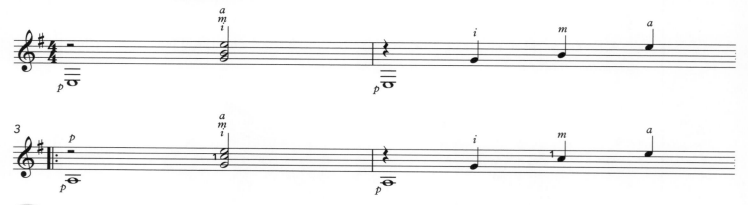

Turn back to pages 18 and 19 and try using these techniques to play the accompanying part of **Green lanes** and **B roads**.

Chord box

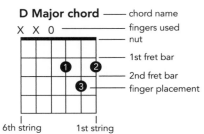

Chord exercise

Play the chords below to prepare for the piece. All left-hand fingerings are shown and the right-hand fingerings are *p* (on all bass notes) and *i m a* on strings 3, 2 and 1 respectively.

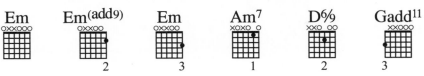

Archipelago arpeggio

*Play **tirando** for this piece.*

molto rall. tells you to slow down a lot.

Quavers (eighth notes)

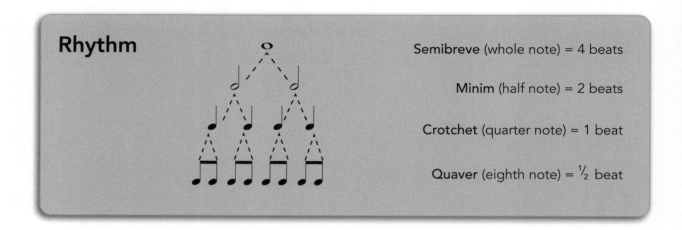

Rhythm

Semibreve (whole note) = 4 beats

Minim (half note) = 2 beats

Crotchet (quarter note) = 1 beat

Quaver (eighth note) = ½ beat

All exercises on this page should be played *apoyando* until secure – then try alternating with *tirando*.

The **C** symbol means 'common time' and is another way of notating a $\frac{4}{4}$ time signature.

Exercise 1

Count: 1   2 + 3   4   1   2 + 3   4   1 + 2 + 3   4   1   2 + 3 + 4

Exercise 2

Count: 1   2   3   1   2 + 3   1   2 + 3 +   1 + 2   3 +

Exercise 3

Count: (1)   2   3   (1)   2 + 3   1   2 + 3 +   1   2 + 3

G major

Count: 1   2 + 3   4   1   2 + 3   4   1   2 + 3   4   1   2   3   4

Freya's quavers

Freya's quavers (accompaniment)

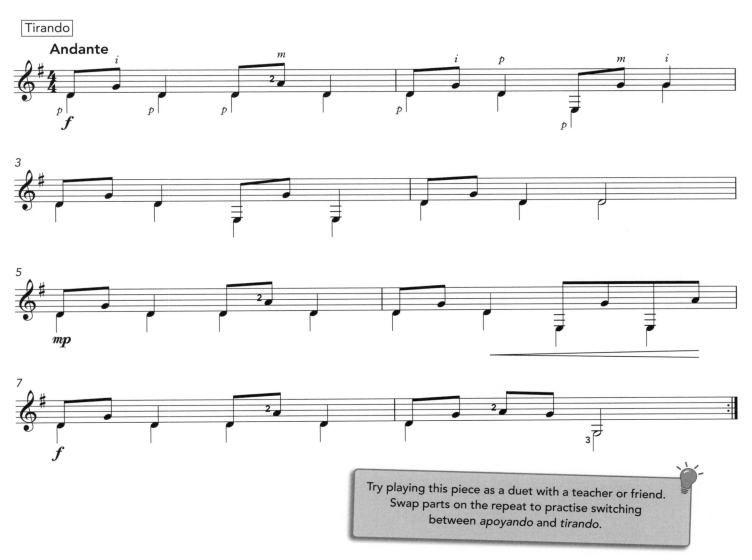

Try playing this piece as a duet with a teacher or friend.
Swap parts on the repeat to practise switching
between *apoyando* and *tirando*.

The following piece alternates *apoyando* with *tirando*. Switching between the two should feel natural due to the shape of the music.

Aveyron

Apoyando
Pluck the string with your index finger then immediately let it rest on the string above.

Preparation   Execution

Tirando
Pluck the string with your index finger then let it move away from the string.

Preparation   Execution

Play the chords in the first exercise in two ways; first with *p i m a* (plant and play) and then strummed with the thumb *p*.

Exercise 1

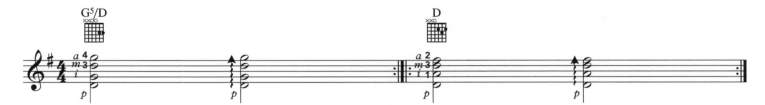

Exercise 2

Promenade

To create a rest after a chord, damp the strings with the little-finger side of the right hand.

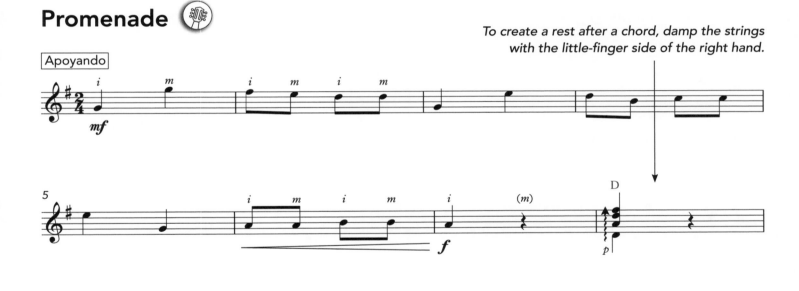

Play the chords with the thumb.

New notes: E, F and B♭

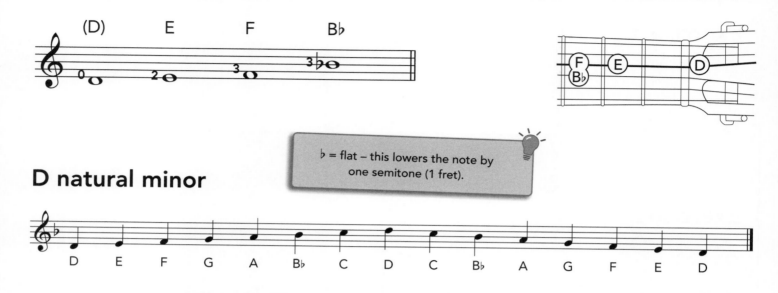

> ♭ = flat – this lowers the note by one semitone (1 fret).

D natural minor

D E F G A B♭ C D C B♭ A G F E D

Despite this scale beginning on string 3, the majority is in the upper strings so *i m* and *apoyando* should be used throughout. This is the same for the next two pieces.

D minor arpeggio

It's all relatively minor

> The *staccato* notes can be performed using the following left-hand technique: release the finger pressure so that the string comes off the fingerboard but the finger stays on the string.

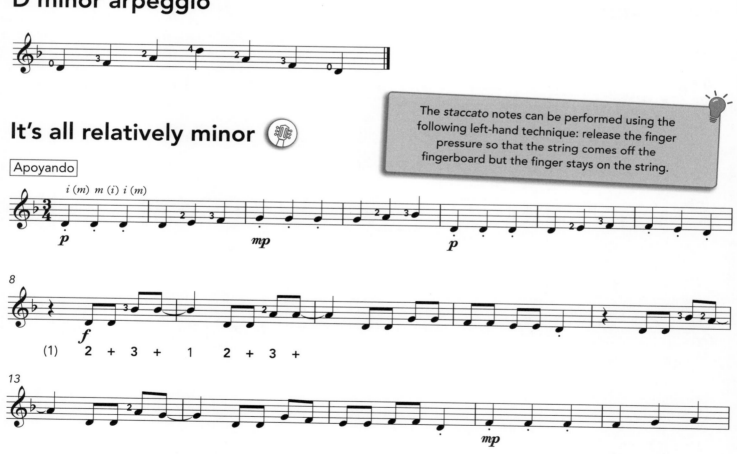

Relatives

As you may have noticed, both D natural minor and F major contain the same notes and have the same key signature; they just start on different notes. The main difference is in their character – the major always sounds happy whereas the minor has a slightly sad feel to it. Each is called the 'relative' of the other.

F major

F   G   A   B♭   C   D   E   F   E   D   C   B♭   A   G   F

It's all relatively major

Apoyando

 This piece can be performed as a duet with **It's all relatively minor**.

New note: F#

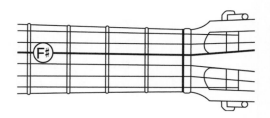

Until now, finger 4 has not played a prominent role, but as the pieces begin to increase in complexity, finger 4 will need to be used more. Often finger 3 will play bass notes and so finger 4 will need to take its place. As with the other fingers, make sure the fingertip and not the pad is used, creating a good arch shape.

Exercise for finger 4

Minuet in G

Christian Petzold (1677–1733)

New note: D♯

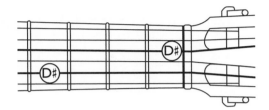

E harmonic minor scale

E F♯ G A B C D♯ E D♯ C B A G F♯ E D♯ E

E minor is the relative of G major – they both have the same key signature of one sharp. There are several different types of minor scale. This harmonic minor scale has a D♯ (raised 7th). You will notice that the D♯ does not appear in the key signature but is written as a separate accidental in the music.

Night creatures

i m – Apoyando
p – Tirando

This bar is an
E minor arpeggio.

Aeolian mode and new notes: B and C

Aeolian mode (A natural minor)

A minor arpeggio

Zach attack

Note there are two contrasting tempos – *tempo primo* indicates that you should return to the original tempo.

New notes: B and C

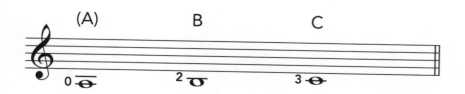

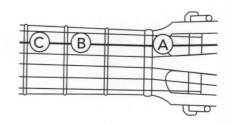

Aeolian mode (A natural minor)

A minor arpeggio

The A minor arpeggio and Aeolian mode scale are the same as on page 36 but an octave lower.

Zach under attack

 Zach attack and Zach under attack can be played as a duet.

This exercise prepares you for playing two notes together. Your fingers should match the 'X' shape shown in the pictures.

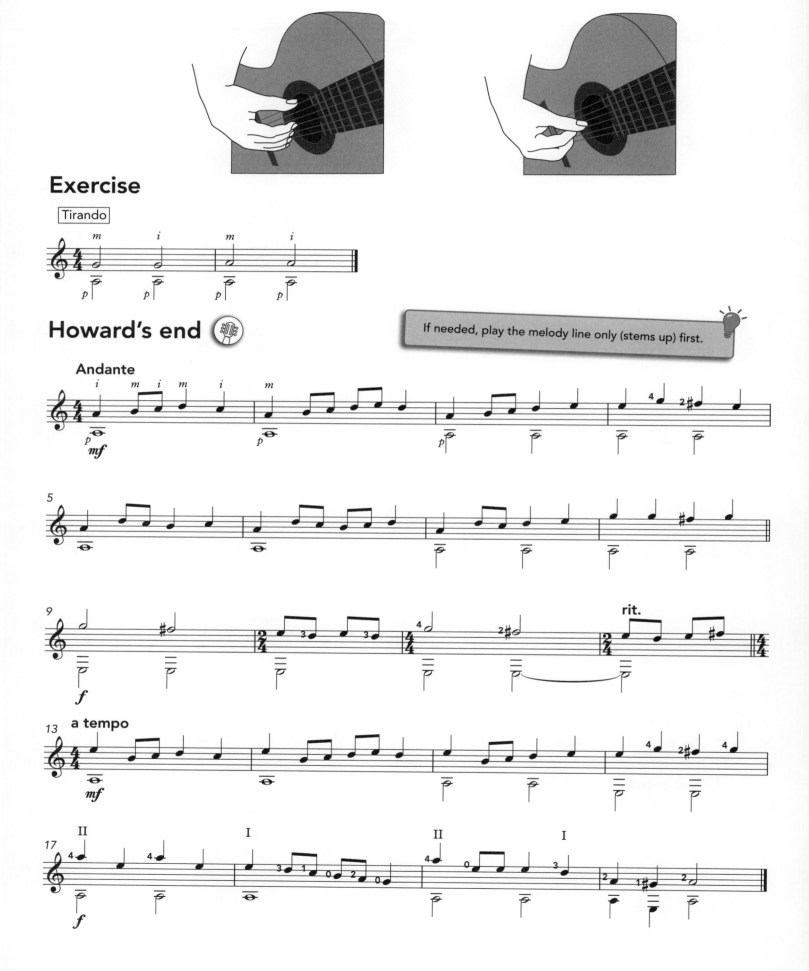

Exercise

Tirando

Howard's end

> If needed, play the melody line only (stems up) first.

Andante

5

9

13 a tempo

17

Dotted notes

Exercise

Apoyando

The dot after the note adds half the value of the original note (𝅗𝅥· = 𝅗𝅥 + ♩). Half the value of a ♩ is a ♪ so ♩· = ♩ + ♪

Count: 1   2   3   4   1 + 2 + 3 + 4 +

1 + 2 + 3 + 4 +   1 + 2 + 3 + 4 +   1 + 2 + 3 + 4 +   1   2   3   4

Theme from New World Symphony

Antonín Dvořák (1841–1904)

Solo Part

Accomp.

The V in bar 30 of *Theme from New World Symphony* signifies the left hand moving into 5th position with finger 1 on fret 5, finger 2 on fret 6 etc. The exercise below is all on string 1 and takes you from 1st position (1st finger on 1st fret) to 3rd position (1st finger on 3rd fret) to 5th position (1st finger on 5th fret).

Position shift exercise

To practise the dotted rhythms, play the melody line (upward stems) first, then play the bass line (all the lower notes) before playing the two parts together.

Ode to joy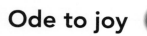

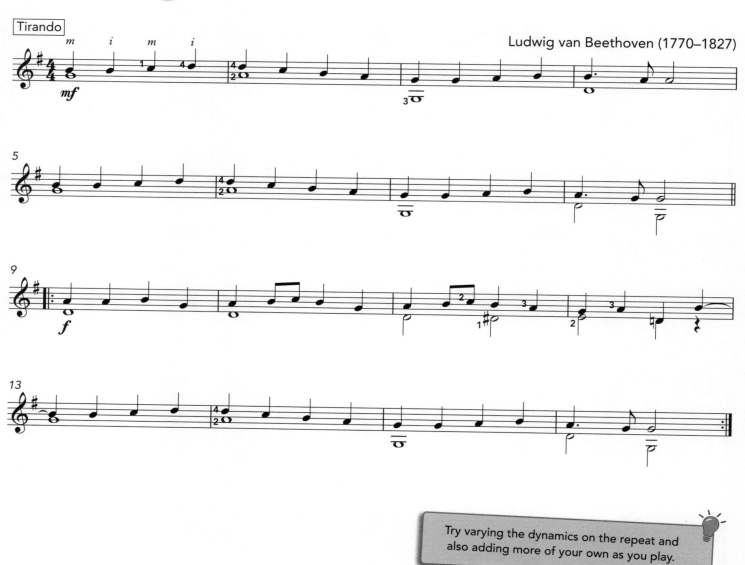

Ludwig van Beethoven (1770–1827)

Try varying the dynamics on the repeat and also adding more of your own as you play.

New note: G♯

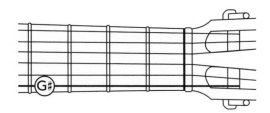

Dotted rhythm exercise in 3/4

Count: 1   2   3   1 + 2 + 3 +   1 + 2 + 3 +   1 + 2 + 3 +

A harmonic minor

A B C D E F G♯ A G♯ F E D C B A G♯ A

Siciliano

Tirando

(2° pont.) *pont. = ponticello (play next to the bridge)*   Matteo Carcassi (1792–1853)

nat. = natural (play normally again)

(2° nat.)

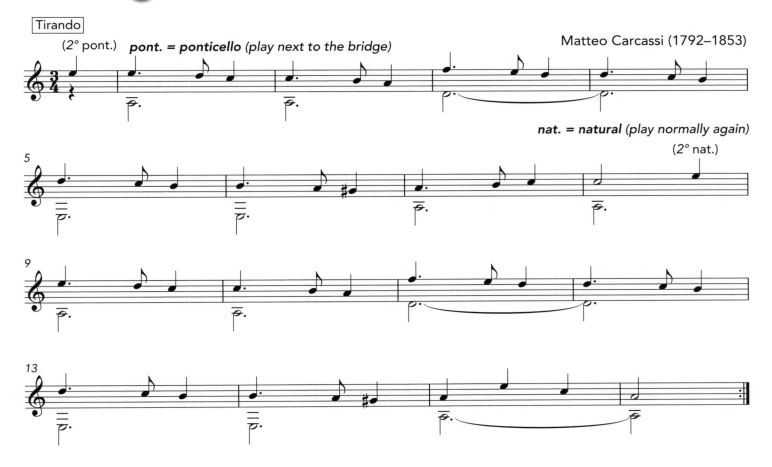

New note: F♯

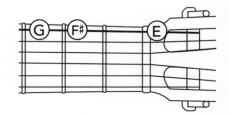

E natural minor

E minor arpeggio

Dark stuff

New note: F

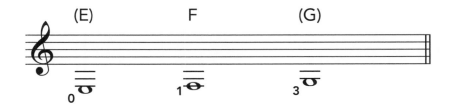

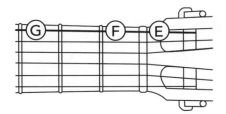

Phrygian mode

E F G A B C D E F G A B C D E D C B A G F E D C B A G F E

Spanish dawn

New notes: B♭ and C♯

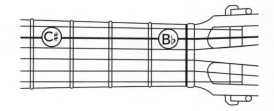

Phrygian dominant mode

Hubbly

Chromatic scale on E

A chromatic scale uses every single note (fret) between two notes with the same name – E and E in the example below.

E   F   F♯   G   G♯   A   A♯   B   C   C♯   D   D♯   E   E♭   D♮   D♭   C♮   B   B♭   A♮   A♭   G♮   G♭   F♮   E

This scale is for the purposes of tuition only, with sharps used in the ascending scale and flats in the descending scale. Whether a note is a G♭ or F♯ depends on which key you are in.

Creepy chromatic

> Try playing along with the guide audio when you feel confident.

Often a slur is used to indicate that a note should be left to ring on beyond its written duration. Here the open strings with slurs should be left to ring on.

The first piece is in the key of A minor and the second is in A major. The two are identical except for the key signature (A minor has all natural notes, whereas A major has three sharps) – the feel of each piece reflects the title.

For help with fingering, take a look at 'A major (2 octaves)' on page 47.

A major second position (II)

Concentrate on being in second position (II) throughout this piece.

Happy (not sad)

This two-octave A major scale is in first position except for the top note.

A major (2 octaves)

Final performance piece

This final piece brings together everything you've learned. Enjoy the contrasting moods and dynamics as you play and try to make the piece your own. Play freely and *sostenuto* until bar 21, and then observe all the rests until the end of the piece to add variety to your performance.

> Refresh your memory of the A harmonic minor scale on page 41 to get you started.

Mr Sinister